In the Power of the Resurrection

Studies on the Book of Acts

Pieter J. Lalleman

In the Power of the Resurrection

Studies on the Book of Acts

Pieter J. Lalleman

WIPF & STOCK · Eugene, Oregon

Wipf and Stock Publishers
199 W 8th Ave, Suite 3
Eugene, OR 97401

In the Power of the Resurrection
Studies on the Book of Acts
By Lalleman, Pieter J.
Copyright©2019 Apostolos
ISBN 13: 978-1-5326-9604-6
Publication date 7/7/2019
Previously published by Apostolos, 2019

Contents

Introduction 8
Chapter One: A Hesitant Start 11
Chapter Two: Money and Possessions 19
Chapter Three: The Conversion of Peter 26
Chapter Four: Cheers, We Have a Sister! 34
Chapter Five: Address in Asia 42
Chapter Six: Prisoner in Europe 50
Chapter Seven: Three Greek Cities 58
Chapter Eight: Acquittal in Corinth 66
Chapter Nine: Exploits in Ephesus 74
Chapter Ten: Free to Proclaim Jesus in Rome 82
Bibliography 89
Other Books by Dr Pieter J. Lalleman 90

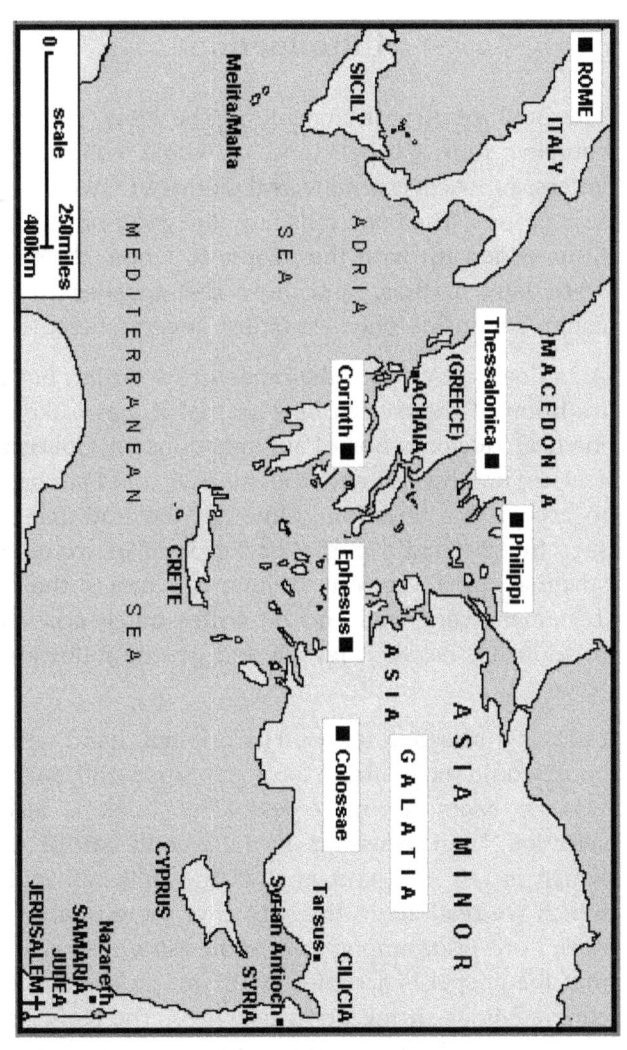

Map by Gordon Smith:
http://www.ccel.org/bible/phillips/JBPhillips.htm

Introduction

The Book of Acts is matchless. The New Testament contains four Gospels and a whole collection of letters, and Acts is unique as the bridge between these two groups. The book tells how the good news about Jesus ended up with the people to whom the letters were later written, and how the apostles formed congregations of followers of Jesus everywhere.

Acts does not contain the name of its writer, but the tradition of the church tells us that it was Luke, the medical doctor whom Paul mentions in Colossians 4:14, 2 Timothy 4:11 and Philemon 24, and I am happy to accept this tradition. Although the tradition also says that he had a pagan background, it would not surprise me if he was a Jew: he knows the Old Testament very well and he writes much about the relationship between Jewish and gentile followers of Jesus.

Luke is a selective writer. His original, hand-written book would have filled a large papyrus scroll, so there was no room for more text. This book is also a selection: I am focussing on the second half of Acts, which is less well-known than the first half and in which we read about the spread of the gospel of the risen Lord Jesus among Jews and gentiles. We will see that the gospel is accepted by many people and that congregations spring up everywhere. The Holy Spirit is at work in liberating and healing many people. Paul always points out how God fulfilled the expectations of Israel. Simultaneously we also see much resistance against the word of God, which takes the form of persecution that regularly results in captivity and even death.

Because Acts is a kind of history book, it is not expected that we as readers indiscriminately imitate everything that is happening in this book. Acts is no ready-to-do lesson pack and we must be careful that we do not perceive everything that happens as a timeless example. More on this in chapter one.

Here follows a little table which indicates the most likely years when the events described occurred:

Event	Chapter in Acts	Year AD
Easter & Pentecost	2	33
Conversion of Paul	9	34 or 35
First 'missionary journey'	13–14	48–49
Second 'missionary journey'	15:36–18:22	50–52
Third 'missionary journey'	18:23–21:16	53–57
Imprisoned in Caesarea	23–26	57–59
Imprisoned in Rome	28	60–62

This book follows the model of my previous book *The Lion and the Lamb* (2016). The Bible passages discussed are sometimes rather long, and so are not reproduced. When you use this book in a group you may not want to read the complete passage aloud. If necessary, use two group meetings to deal with the material. Because of the length of the passages, not every detail in the text is discussed.

Pieter J. Lalleman

Chapter One: A Hesitant Start

Acts 1

Introduction and Background Information

i. Acts show what it means that the kingdom of God has come. It was brought by the Lord Jesus, who now reigns in heaven. His place is taken by the Holy Spirit, for God continues his plan and sends his Spirit to lead and to help the followers of Jesus. The kingdom extends as far as Rome and subsequently it must reach the ends of the earth.

ii. In Antiquity, long texts were distributed over various 'books', exactly as Luke is doing here. The 'Gospel according to Luke' is his first volume about Jesus and this is his second. A book's introduction acted as a kind of back cover text and it was the place to refer back to any previous volume. Like the first volume, this second volume is dedicated to Theophilus (cf. Luke 1:3), about whom we know nothing more.

iii. Luke begins his second book with a more elaborate description of Jesus' ascension than he had given in Luke 24. In this way the ascension forms the hinge between the two volumes. Historically, for the followers of Jesus it is the beginning of a time of waiting for the Spirit. They have received Jesus' commission but they are not yet allowed to begin the work. Yet they are not idle.

iv. Verses 15–26 are written in the style of the Old Testament, as if Luke wants to emphasise that the first followers of Jesus are all Jews. See for example the expression 'to go in and out' (verse 21, NRSV), which in the NIV has become 'to live among us'.

v. This chapter immediately shows clearly that not everything Luke tells us is worthy of imitation. As I explained in the Introduction, Luke tells us what happened without expressing approval or disapproval.

vi. The chapter can be divided into verses 1–3, 4–11 and 12–26.

Explanation of the Text

1:1–2 Luke refers back to the book we know as 'the Gospel according to Luke'. His words mean that he is now going to describe the continuation of the deeds and teaching of Jesus. In other words, the Lord Jesus will also be central to this second volume. After him the apostles are introduced.

1:3 From the beginning Luke puts the resurrection of Jesus at the centre; everywhere in Acts we hear about this important event. There are many eyewitnesses of the resurrection so that no-one can deny it. It was more than a vision!

1:3, 6 The kingdom of God has an important place in the Gospels. In Acts it occurs far less, but Luke mentions it here and at the end of the book, among other places. This makes clear that it is still an important theme. The kingdom of God is not a geographical area and it does not merely coincide with the church either; it is something that happens when people follow and obey Jesus. God's will is done in his church and throughout the earth – at present imperfectly, in the future in perfect fashion.

1:4–5 From here the story is pointing forward. We read about the promise of the Spirit in Luke 12:12 and John 14:15–26; 16:7–15. Sometimes the expression 'baptism' (cf. 11:16) is used for what is otherwise called 'receiving the Spirit' (2:38; 8:15) or 'being filled with the Spirit' (2:4; 4:31; 9:17). In the Bible there is no difference in meaning between these phrases.

1:6–7 It seems that Jesus does not give his followers a direct answer to their question, but the answer is 'yes'. At that time God was already restoring his kingdom; his ancient people Israel was being extended by the inclusion of believers from the nations. At his ascension, Jesus formally took his place on the throne, and his followers must pass on this news. However, it is not the kind of kingdom for which the disciples might have hoped, because they do not immediately receive a beautiful throne and a good life in heaven. God has the 'authority' in the world (verse 7) and the followers will receive 'power' (verse 8) for their role as witnesses, heralds of his kingdom. The kingdom is where they – and we – recognise Jesus as Lord.

1:8 Jesus' words are based on Isaiah 49:6. A witness is someone who speaks on the basis of personal experience. The expression 'the ends of the earth' does not refer to Rome, because that city was the *centre* of the then world. For the people in the Roman Empire, Spain, Ethiopia, India and the territory of the Germans were the boundaries of the known world. Thus the command of Jesus was not yet completely carried out during the period described in Acts.

1:9–11 Luke's description of Jesus' departure in terms of going up does not need to trouble us who know that the earth is a sphere and that God's place of residence is not simply 'above'. The promise that Jesus will come back still holds true. For the moment he sends some angels to help his perplexed followers.

1:12 Only now Luke tells that the ascension took place from the Mount of Olives. A Sabbath day's walk is the distance that a Jew can travel according to the rules of the Pharisees without doing 'work' on the Sabbath (e.g. Exodus 20:10; Leviticus 23:3), about three-quarters of a mile. Luke adds this detail to indicate that Jesus departed from Jerusalem.

1:13 This is possibly the same upper room where Jesus had celebrated the last supper with the disciples (Luke 22:12); the owner was probably also a follower of the Lord. In any case the group of Galileans finds a quiet place of residence here.

1:14 From the beginning Luke puts emphasis on the strong fellowship among the believers. Prayer is always good, but certainly when the way forward is not yet clear. Among the women are probably the ones that Luke mentioned in Luke 8:1–3 and 23:55–24:10.

1:15 The timing is vague; this event occurs on one of the days between the ascension and the day of Pentecost. Luke has not reported that Peter had formally taken the leadership of the group, and Peter is probably acting fairly impulsively (cf. Luke 9:33; 22:33; 24:12). The Jewish tradition required the presence of 120 persons to form a new community. It is also understandable that the number of twelve was valued because it symbolises the people of Israel (e.g. Exodus 24:4; 28:21; 39:14).

1:16 As the footnote in the NIV indicates, the original Greek text has 'brothers' (cf. ESV, KJV). This word normally has an inclusive meaning, so the translation 'brothers and sisters' is accurate.

Peter probably refers to Psalm 41:9, 'Even my close friend, whom I trusted, he who shared my bread, has lifted up his heel against me.' He does not need to quote the text, for his audience would have known it. The Hebrew scriptures help them to understand what had happened.

1:17 Judas had fully been part of the group – his action and his death were very painful for the others.

1:18–19 Here Luke interrupts Peter to tell the prehistory. The brackets have been added by the NIV translators. Matthew 27:1–10 contains other details, which are difficult to fit with Luke's words. Judas had apparently bought a piece of land, but this detail is not recorded in Luke's Gospel. The Jewish population had already given a nickname to this piece of land.

1:20 Peter quotes Psalm 69:25 to proclaim a vacancy and Psalm 109:8 to declare that it must be fulfilled. He uses the Greek translation, which is slightly different from the Hebrew text of the Old Testament.

1:21–22 Here we see again how important the resurrection was to the first community. An apostle speaks in the first place about the resurrection of the Lord. But the question is whether Peter is right that another apostle must already be chosen. That this happens before the Holy Spirit has come is probably an error on the part of the congregation. Matthias is never heard of again later, and did God not have Paul in mind already? Moreover, the way in which the appointment takes place, by casting lots, is not something that we must imitate. The requirement that this person should be an eyewitness to Jesus is justified. The required person must be a man because women were not acceptable as witnesses under Jewish law.

1:23 Both men are otherwise unknown to us.

1:26 Greeks and other Jews also used lots to make decisions, for example in order to compile rota (Luke 1:9). How the casting of lots went exactly, we don't know, but the procedure basically gave God a free hand.

Application

1. Jesus' return to heaven means more than that he is gone. It is a vital element of the faith because he is now reigning as king on the throne next to God (cf.

Revelation 3:21; 22:1, 3). Luke says little about the meaning of the ascension, but in Acts 2:33–36 Peter calls it Jesus' exaltation. In Hebrews 1:3–4 it is seen as evidence of Jesus' superiority over the angels (and thus over all creation) and in Hebrews 8:1 and 12:2 (cf. Ephesians 1:20-23) the emphasis is on Jesus' sovereignty. The ascended Lord is the giver of the Spirit (Ephesians 4:8).

2. Acts tells us what happened, but not everything in history is an example to us. Throughout the Bible we must distinguish between doctrinal parts (like the Letters) and narrative parts (such as Judges and Kings). The Bible is authoritative – but not everything is normative for us. An extreme example of bad behaviour is what Ananias and Sapphira did (5:1–11), but elsewhere in Luke's story we must also ask ourselves whether an event is normative. Often Bible writers such as Luke do make comments that provide guidance for us; in the absence of any such comment, repetition is also a good indication that an act is in accordance with God's will.

3. The apostles' unique position was that they had been eyewitnesses to the risen Lord. Therefore, in later times there are virtually no churches which label their leaders as apostles. Leaders are needed, but present-day leaders do not have the absolute authority of the apostles.

For Thought and Discussion

1. What does it mean for us that Jesus is seated on the throne?
2. How do you deal with a worldview in which Jesus ascends to heaven?
3. For us, where are 'the ends of the earth'? Are they far away?
4. How does your church appoint leaders? Is there any biblical support for doing it this way? What role does prayer have in the procedure?
5. Can we regard the Bible as the successor of the apostles when it comes to testimony regarding the resurrection of Jesus?
6. What role do believers today have as witnesses to Jesus?

Chapter Two: Money and Possessions

Acts 2:42–47, 4:31–5:11

Introduction and Background Information

i. This chapter combines discussions of parts of Acts 2, 4 and 5. These passages first give us a clear picture of how the first Christians lived, and then focus specifically on the subject of money and other possessions. How did the first followers of Jesus handle these things and is this in any way relevant for us?

ii. In chapter one we saw that not everything Luke tells us is normative, but his summaries of the life of the first congregation certainly are. These summaries show us what the normal practices of the believers looked like and how God blessed them. They show us how following Jesus changes people and they can be models for us. In Acts 2:42–47, 4:32–35 and 5:12–16 we find such summaries. Acts 4:32–35 is followed by a diptych of two contrasting stories: one about Barnabas (4:36–37) and one about Ananias and Sapphira (5:1–11).

iii. Luke stresses the common meals of the believers. In many cultures the meal is the central moment of fellowship and the highlight of the day. In addition, in the Old Testament it is also an image of God's coming redemption (Isaiah 25:6–8, cf. Revelation 19:9).

iv. All divisions between passages and all headers in modern translations are additions by the translators;

as such they can be ignored. In this case, it is useful to take 4:31 with the following verses, see below.

Explanation of the Text

2:42 The word 'teaching' does not yet refer to a complete system of doctrine, because that was not yet available. As in Peter's speeches, the teaching of the apostles will have focused on the Hebrew scriptures, our Old Testament. The 'breaking of bread' was probably part of a normal meal, as is suggested by verse 46 and 1 Corinthians 11:20–22.

2:43 Thanks to the many 'wonders and signs' outsiders have great respect for the church; they find the power of God awe-inspiring but see also verse 47.

2:44–45 Luke introduces a further characteristic of the congregation: the members live closely together, and they share their possessions; property is also sold so that the money can be used to care for the needy. At that time this practice also took place in some Jewish groups, which may have inspired the congregation. In 4:32–35 it becomes clear that the selling and distribution happened voluntarily.

2:46 There were obviously no church buildings yet – these were only built after the year 200 and until then the Christians met in existing buildings. The vast squares around the temple building were a convenient meeting place for large groups; the followers of Jesus probably also participated in the daily thank-offerings in the inner temple.

2:47 Here we see three things. Firstly, the lifestyle of the first Christians, good as it was, did not focus on themselves but on God. Secondly, they were seen and respected, they 'found favour' with outsiders. This led to the third, which is that God was able to add ever more new people to the congregation; indeed every day!

***

4:31 This verse has a bridge function. It rounds off the preceding section which relates the release of Peter and John from prison and the response of the congregation. At the same time, it is also the beginning of the next section, as is indicated by the form of the Greek word for 'spoke', which points to a habit. The congregation asks for boldness to speak about Jesus and they are again filled with the Holy Spirit. It is the Spirit who enables them to live as described in verses 32–35.

4:32 The Holy Spirit first and foremost gives unity. Luke here uses words which were used by Greeks and other gentiles to describe an ideal society. The effect of the unity is that believers no longer cling to their private property.

4:33 This is a wonderful summary of the proclamation of the apostles! They are the eyewitnesses of the resurrection because they had seen the risen Lord, only a few months before. The Greek words in this verse once again point to a lasting habit.

4:34–35 Luke repeats what he wrote in 2:44–45, and in so doing he gives extra emphasis and endorsement to the 'community of goods'. The wording makes clear that he is alluding to Deuteronomy 15:4 and 7 as well as to pagan literature, in which the absence of poverty is a blessing.

We do not know for certain why here and in 5:2 the feet of the apostles are specifically mentioned; it could be a legal convention.

4:36–37 Barnabas is named as an example of someone who acts as described in verses 32–35. He also serves as a foil for Ananias and Sapphira. At the same time Luke introduces him because he will play an important role later in the story (from 11:22). He will turn out to be first a great mentor and then a loyal travelling companion for Paul.

5:1–11 Several supernatural things take place here: Peter knows what Ananias and Sapphira had really done; and both of them die suddenly. The deaths may have been due to the shock of the unexpected discovery of their clever plan. No wonder that both believers and outsiders are very impressed (verse 11).

Unlike Ananias, Sapphira is clearly given the opportunity to confess her sin, but she does not grasp the opportunity (verse 8).

You might wonder why the lie of Ananias and Sapphira was so bad. The problem is that they speak falsely without any reason, unprovoked, and they damage the quality of life in the congregation. They threaten to introduce hypocrisy into God's people, giving God's opponents an inroad. Peter calls their wickedness a lie to the Holy Spirit. Note that we are merely told about their temporary punishment but not about their eternal fate; about the latter only God knows.

Application

1. Acts 2:42–47 and 4:31–35 can be summarised as 'love God above all and your neighbour as yourself' (cf. Luke 10:27) and – in modern terms the gospel runs counter-culturally against the prevailing ideas of individualism. Luke describes an ideal situation which was inspired by the Holy Spirit. People love seeing each other, both in the temple and at home. The every-day life of the congregation brings joy from heaven to earth, even though we are informed that it was impossible to keep sin outside.

2. Once again the highlight in the life of the believers is identified as having a meal together. Relaxation after exertion. They praise the Lord together. He gives himself to us, and he gives us to each other.

3. Readiness to share possessions is a repeated theme in Acts (cf. also 9:36–42) and this indicates without a doubt that God approved of the practice. This should not surprise us because it was Jesus himself who often spoke about money and possessions: almost half of Luke 9–19 is concerned with this subject. The first congregation of his followers applied his teaching to their situation and we should do the same to our

situation. Faithfulness to the gospel leads to a wise and generous use of money and goods. The gospel should not only influence us to offer our lives to God, but also our wallets!

Yet note that this is not a situation of imposed equality, but of voluntary sharing and the prevention of poverty. Thus it is not Communism, in which the freedom of people is restricted. There were still people who owned houses and other things, and who were using them to good effect (cf. 12:12).

4. The story of Ananias and Sapphira is the hardest in the Book of Acts. It shows how God hates deliberate sins and how under the new covenant he still sets high standards for life in the church. At the same time the sudden death of this couple is a one-off event. Later in the New Testament we still come across serious sins (1 Corinthians 5:1; 2 Timothy 4:14; James 2:6–7; 1 John 4:3), but God does not again interfere to punish these. Thus the death of Ananias and Sapphira illustrates the fact that under the new covenant God's norms are no lower than under the old covenant (cf. Matthew 5:20–48). But he only shows this once, thankfully. Until the last judgement he mercifully tolerates our trespasses. This interpretation makes the present story, which takes place at the very beginning of the history of the church, a close parallel to the story of the flood at the beginning of world history (Genesis 6–9).

For Thought and Discussion

1. Acts 2:42 mentions three things that are important for a congregation. How much attention do these three things get in your congregation and why?

2. According to 4:33, the apostles mainly mentioned the resurrection of Jesus. Should they not have spoken about the cross above all?

3. Do you think that the Lord can add people to the congregation (as in 2:47) if the church has a bad reputation? What does this mean in your situation?

4. Nowadays learning about God and the Bible, listening to the teaching of 'apostles', is not very popular. How could we change this?

5. Do you agree with the above explanation of the death of Ananias and Sapphira? Do you think that God acted justly or was he too strict?

6. Do you agree with the view expressed above that the community of goods was not only an ideal for the first congregation, but also for us? If so, are you likely to take action to achieve this ideal? How much control do you allow God to have over your money and possessions?

Chapter Three: The Conversion of Peter

Acts 10

Introduction and Background Information

i. Up to this moment in the story, the gospel has only been shared with Jews and Samaritans – with the exception of the lonely courtier in Acts 8. Will the apostles ever begin to carry out Jesus' assignment as given in 1:8? Yes, but even in the present chapter they do not act on their own initiative. God has to intervene by means of two visions and in Acts 11 Peter has to explain himself in face of the other believers who distrust his actions. The first step towards the gentiles which is being taken here is so important that Luke describe it extensively, and in 11:5–17 he repeats the essentials; see also 15:7–9.

ii. The story contains various parallels between Cornelius and Peter: both are praying and both are subsequently prepared to do the will of God by means of a vision. This underlines how difficult this step outside his comfort zone was for Peter.

iii. Anyone who knows the Old Testament can observe that Luke also includes various parallels between Jonah and Peter. Both men are located in the coastal town of Joppa (modern-day Jaffa). Both are sent to a gentile audience in order to convey God's Word, but they do not want to do so at all. In both cases God interferes and overcomes the resistance of his servant.

iv. Verses 34–43 contain Peter's only speech to non-Jews and his last in Acts. This chapter consists of the following elements:

Cornelius needs Peter (1–8).

Peter does not want to go to Cornelius (9–20).

Peter meets Cornelius (21–33).

Peter speaks about Jesus (34–43).

Cornelius becomes a follower of Jesus (44–48).

Explanation of the Text

10:1–2 The Roman army which occupied Israel consisted of soldiers not only from Italy but also from many other countries. To distinguish it from other regiments, that of Cornelius is called Italian.

At that time numerous gentiles served the God of Israel, especially in the country of Israel; they are often called proselytes. We can see that Cornelius had not taken the step to become a proselyte from the fact that he was not circumcised (11:3). The story also suggests that he did not keep a *kosher* diet. He therefore belongs to the group of so-called 'Godfearers', but he distinguishes himself positively by his lifestyle. In this respect he resembles the Roman officer in Luke 7:1–10.

10:3–5 It is remarkable that a gentile sees a vision from God. The Greek text has 'the ninth hour' and NIV provides a correct interpretation rather than a translation. Three o'clock in the afternoon was the time of the afternoon prayer, see 3:1. The normal human reaction to seeing an angel is fright – and therefore angels usually begin by putting people at ease. Verse 4 suggests that God has received Cornelius' prayers and gifts as a voluntary sacrifice. The angel does not tell Cornelius why Peter should visit him.

10:6 Simon Peter is staying with Simon the tanner, as 9:43 told us. Luke makes things complicated by referring to Peter as Simon is verses 5, 18 and 19.

10:7–8 Cornelius obeys the strange command.

10:9–10 God begins to prepare Peter for a meeting with Cornelius. The Greek text has 'the sixth hour' and NIV again provides an interpretation rather than a translation. Anyway, midday was not a normal mealtime in Israel so Peter's hunger is unnatural. The vision he is about to see is a kind of parable that will require explanation.

10:12, 14 The law on unclean animals is in Leviticus 11 and Peter wants to obey it. His words are based on Ezekiel 4:14.

10:13, 15 God declares all animals clean; this implies that Peter can visit the home of a non-Jew like Cornelius and sit at the table. The Lord Jesus had said more or less the same thing in Mark 7:18–19, but the meaning of his teaching had not yet been understood by the church. Of course the deeper meaning of the vision is that God declares all human beings clean.

Therefore Peter can and must respond positively to the imminent request of Cornelius.

10:16 His dogged loyalty to the food laws makes Peter deaf to God's progressing revelation. God is required to state what he means three times.

10:17–20 The situation for which God has prepared Peter immediately presents itself.

10:20 Here (and in 11:12) the Greek word translated as 'do not hesitate' also has the nuance of 'without distinction'. The Holy Spirit has to repeat once more what Peter has just learned. Here it says that it is the Spirit who has sent the messengers, while in verses 4–8 it is an angel. Of course this is no contradiction, as the Spirit had made use of an angel.

10:22 This sums up the verses 1–5.

10:23 Peter receives the three men into the house, although they are probably non-Jewish and despite the fact that he does not own the house. It seems that he is beginning to understand the meaning of the vision.

10:24 The distance between the two coastal towns is some 30 miles. Cornelius' friends and relatives are gentiles, see verse 45.

10:25–26 Falling at someone's feet is a normal custom of reverence among both Jews and gentiles. But the Greek text implies that Cornelius intends a form of worship which is rightly rejected by Peter.

10:28 Peter openly mentions the hurdle of exclusivity he had to overcome and the lesson he has learned in Joppa.

10:30–33a Cornelius repeats what we know from the verses 3–8.

10:33b Cornelius has high expectations of Peter's words.

10:34–35 Peter begins his speech by explicitly opening the door to gentiles, thus showing that he understands the meaning of his vision. He must do what God also does: accept every person. God has no special friends.

10:36 The promise of peace comes from Jeremiah 33:6. Note the tension: the word came through the people of Israel – but Jesus is Lord of all people.

10:37–41 Peter briefly states the main facts about Jesus: he is the Christ (Messiah, God's servant) and Lord (highest authority). Filled with the Spirit he worked in Israel, he died and rose again. 'With the Holy Spirit and power' (verse 38) means 'with the power of the Holy Spirit'. This verse shows that Jesus did more than merely die on the cross; his life on earth also had enormous value. Verse 39 does not specify who were responsible for the crucifixion of Jesus. On the witnesses of the resurrection, see also 1 Corinthians 15:5–8 and Luke 24:10, 33–36.

10:42 The penultimate element of Peter's words is the declaration that God has appointed Jesus 'as judge of the living and the dead'. This is a slightly veiled reference to a possible punishment for unbelief.

10:43 The prophets of Israel's only get a brief mention because their words were largely unknown to gentiles. Even so, Peter probably has Isaiah 53 foremost in mind, see also Daniel 9:24. His speech ends on a positive note, with an offer of forgiveness for anyone who believes. In Jewish parlance the 'name' means the person themselves.

10:44–46 Luke does not always tell us that new believers receive the Holy Spirit and speak in new languages. Here he does, and the report suggests that the miracle of Pentecost is being repeated. The reason for being explicit at this point is that this is the first time that a group of gentiles comes to faith. From the outset it must be crystal clear that these people have the same status as believers with a Jewish background and that they are in no way second-class members of the church. And this is not a human decision either: it is the Holy Spirit who declares it in an indisputable way!

The expression used in the original Greek is 'speaking in tongues'; as the note in the NIV indicates, this is normally understood as speaking in foreign languages.

10:47–48 In the New Testament repentance (conversion) and baptism belong closely together. As the Spirit has already come, baptism is the reasonable human response. It is striking that no baptismal instruction is given. The people who had travelled with Peter (verse 23; 11:12) act as witnesses.

Application

1. We may not often reflect on this, but the church is open to everyone! In Ephesians 2:11–22 Paul explains this to believers from a gentile background. Peter and the other Jewish believers still had to be convinced of this. But let us not be too critical of them. In the era of slavery most Christians failed to understand that slaves are also sisters and brothers. In the same way in which Peter wanted to maintain the separation between clean and unclean animals, today, we are challenged to include as equals in our churches people from every race, colour and culture.

2. Our practice does not always keep pace with our beliefs. In our time many churches still only accommodate one kind of people. In a multi-ethnic society, this does not do justice to God's purposes. Moreover, the church should also be inclusive in terms of social class and age groups.

3. In every respect Cornelius is a good person – yet he too needs Jesus. For the good and benevolent people around us this implies that it is not sufficient to lead a good life. They too must turn around and find life in Jesus. Yet note that between verses 43 and 44 there is nothing about consciousness of sin, repentance and so on. The Holy Spirit apparently knows what is going on in the hearts of Cornelius and the people around him. The combination of the threat of judgement and

the offer of forgiveness in verses 42–43 shows that everyone both can and must become a Christian.

For Thought and Discussion

1. Who is converted in this story?

2. The normal human reaction to seeing an angel is fright – and therefore angels usually begin by putting people at ease. How many examples of this pattern can you find in the Bible?

3. Verse 34 continues to be a challenge, especially for Christians, because they are not supposed to put their own people first. In the Majority World the church is growing. Do we treat everyone in the same way, without hesitation and without making any undue distinctions?

4. Culture and cultural differences keep people apart. Do you notice that in the behaviour of others? And how is that with you? Is it ever right to keep a distance?

5. Have you been baptised? If not, why not?

6. Which songs and hymns do you know about the theme of this chapter?

7. Identify who does what in this story: God, Jesus, the Holy Spirit, Cornelius, Peter.

Chapter Four: Cheers, We Have a Sister!

Acts 11:19–30 and 13:1–3

Introduction

i. It had taken a while before the gospel message had managed to get outside the walls of Jerusalem, but now that the first steps have been taken, it is moving fast. It is the Greek-speaking Jews who take the initiative. The foundation of the church in Antioch is of invaluable significance for the growth of Christianity. We read about the origins of this local congregation (11:19–26), about the assistance they give to Jerusalem (11:27–30) and about the beginning of the first organised 'mission' – not caused by the pressure of persecution as it had been before (13:1–3). Barnabas and Paul are beginning to take over as the main characters of Luke's story.

ii. In the 2011 edition of the NIV, 12:25 is treated as the beginning of a new passage. Earlier versions of the NIV and most other translations take 12:25 as the conclusion of the preceding passage. As I said in chapter two, the division of the text and the addition of headings are the work of modern translators.

Background Information

i. Antioch was one of the largest cities of the Roman Empire, with perhaps 500,000 inhabitants, many more than Jerusalem. The city had a mixed population, with a large Jewish minority. Antioch was situated in a strategic position, it had good connections in all directions and it was the capital of the Roman province of Syria. Later on, we will see that the local congregation of followers of Jesus did not keep the Jewish laws (15:1–2); this decision was of decisive significance for the entire church in subsequent times.

Phoenicia (verse 19, see also 15:3 and 21:2) is roughly modern-day Lebanon. Cyrene (verse 20) is in North Africa.

ii. The form of the word 'Christians' (11:26) suggests that it had a Latin background, which indicates that it had been coined by Latin speakers. It means 'followers of Christ', so it is not a bad label. The only problem is that it gives the impression that Christ was taken as a proper name, while it is actually a title which means Messiah, 'anointed one'.

It is noteworthy that Luke himself seems to avoid the word Christians, as in the New Testament it only appears in Acts 26:28 and 1 Peter 4:16, where it shows how outsiders spoke about the believers. Hence originally it was not a self-designation and Luke prefers to use 'The Way' instead (cf. 9:2; 18:25–26; 19:9, 23; 22:4; 24:14, 22).

iii. In Galatians 2:1–10 Paul describes the same visit to Jerusalem which is mentioned in Acts 11:30, albeit his report has a different emphasis to Luke.

iv. 'Herod the Tetrarch' who is mentioned in 13:1 is otherwise known as Herod Antipas, the person who reigned over Galilee from 4 BC to AD 39 (cf. Matthew

14:1–9; Luke 3:1, 19–20; 8:3; 23:6–12). He was a son of Herod the Great, the child murderer of Bethlehem. As a contemporary of this ruler, Manaen must be at least 60 years of age. The Jewish name Manaen (Menachem) means 'comforter'.

v. In between his later travels Paul returned to Jerusalem, but he also visited Antioch each time (14:26–28; 18:22–23). Therefore we might call the Antioch congregation his home church.

vi. In the Bible the laying-on of hands occurs in many places and on various occasions, but not as often as you might think. It symbolises transferring blessing and strength. In Genesis 48:13–16, Jacob lays his hands on two of his grandsons to bless them. The laying-on of hands also took place with all kinds of sacrifices (Leviticus 1:4, 3:2, etc.) and in a negative sense when transferring sins onto a sacrificial animal (Leviticus 4:24).

The Lord Jesus sometimes laid his hands on people, for example when he blessed children (Matthew 19:13–15) and when performing some healings (Mark 6:5; Luke 4:40). In Acts the apostles lay hands on the seven helpers (6:6). The laying-on of hands was a way of conveying the Holy Spirit (Acts 8:15–17) or certain gifts (1 Timothy 4:14; 2 Timothy 1:6).

Explanation of the Text

11:19 Luke here picks up the thread which he had let go in 8:2–4. The persecution of the congregation in Jerusalem has an unexpected and positive effect: at last these believers are moving out into the world. Yet for the moment the Aramaic-speaking Jewish followers of Jesus only speak to fellow Jews about the gospel ('the word').

11:20–21 The Greek-speaking Jewish believers from Cyprus and Cyrene do better: they make contact with people of a non-Jewish background (verse 20) and they see much fruit from that work. This means that for the first time many gentiles come to faith.

11:22 The church in Jerusalem had always shown an interest in what was happening elsewhere, see 8:14 and 11:1–3. As a Cypriot (4:36), Barnabas was a suitable representative, who was open to God's work in new circumstances. He may have volunteered for this role.

11:23–24 Barnabas becomes a kind of minister (pastor) in Antioch and the growth of the congregation continues steadily. He lives up to his name of 'comforter' or 'encourager' (4:36) and Luke is very positive about his character.

11:25 After his conversion Saul had ended up in his hometown of Tarsus (9:30), which was not far from Antioch. He had been there for at least ten years, yet Luke never tells us what he had been doing during that time. But now Barnabas needs assistance and goes in search of his former pupil (9:27). At this moment and until 13:7 Barnabas is the most important of the pair, for he is always mentioned first. Luke here does not even mention Saul's response to the request of his mentor.

11:26 Luke gives few details about the passing of time, but here he shows that Barnabas and Saul take time to give the congregation a solid foundation.

11:27 It is unclear what exactly the role of 'prophets' was at that time. They are also mentioned in 13:1 and 15:32, but nowhere else. (In many other places the word refers to the prophets of the Old Covenant.) Nor does Luke explain who 'the elders' in Jerusalem (verse 30) are, or what exactly their role was. By this time most of the twelve apostles had probably gone out into the world to proclaim the gospel and these elders would be the new local leaders. In any case, the term 'elder' is more an indication of spiritual status than of age.

11:28 During the reign of the Emperor Claudius (AD 41–54) there were several famines that made it into the history books. The Greek text has 'the whole world' but the NIV has rendered this as 'the entire Roman world'.

11:29–30 Apparently the congregation in Antioch was more affluent than the one in Jerusalem. This may have been caused by the fact that in Israel the Sabbath-years continued to be observed (Leviticus 25:1–7) and the famine may have come at a vulnerable moment. However this may be, the new congregation now has the opportunity to do something for the first congregation. This is the first example of a congregation helping another congregation; the second congregation helps the first; daughter helps mother.

***

13:1 Luke gives five names, which point to a very mixed leadership team. Simeon is a Jewish name. Niger is a Latin name that means 'black'; like Paul this man has two names. Lucius came from Cyrene in North Africa. These five persons were probably representative of the diversity of the church in Antioch. The Roman Empire was a class society, but in the congregation such differences appear to be irrelevant.

13:2 The church is spiritually united, just like the church in Jerusalem. This enables the Holy Spirit to address them effectively – Luke does not tell us how. Fasting (not eating, sometimes also drinking little) is prescribed in the Old Testament, but is not made obligatory in the New Testament. It is intended to enable people to show their dedication to God and to have closer contact with God than would otherwise be possible.

13:3 The congregation obeys the clear guidance of the Spirit. (In this verse it is the congregation that acts, in verse 4 it says that it is the Holy Spirit. That is not a contradiction – they were working together.) Thus, Barnabas and Paul are sent out a second time (cf. 11:30), but now for a longer period of time. Luke emphasizes the fact that they constitute two of the five leaders of the congregation, that is 40 per cent of the leadership is being sent out! Laying-on of hands conveys God's blessing to them.

Application

1. Luke clearly shows the tremendous solidarity between the first two congregations, despite their obvious differences which come to the fore in Acts 15. His description of the church in Antioch is clearly intended as an example for his readers past and present.

2. A role reversal takes place between Jerusalem and Antioch. In our time we see something similar between the church in the West and the church in the Majority World. This could be God's provision for the future of his church.

3. The church in Antioch shows great willingness to make significant sacrifices both at the spiritual and the material level. Because they do not cling to their leaders Barnabas and Saul, they open the way for the further spreading of the message about Jesus, about which we read in the following chapters.

For Thought and Discussion

1. Read the following verses and note how Luke calls the followers of Jesus: 1:15; 2:41, 44; 4:32; 8:1; 9:1, 2, 31; 11:1; 12:1, 5; 19:9, 23; 24:14. Consult different translations. How does Paul refer to them in his letters?

2. Is it possible that Saul felt more at home in the church of Antioch than in Jerusalem? Why would that be?

3. In what ways do you see the church in Antioch as an example for your own situation? Are there also things you cannot imitate?

4. Is it practically possible to release leaders of your congregation for other work? Would there also be other ways in which you could stimulate the spread of the gospel? How about church planting?

5. Do you know examples of partnership between different congregations?

6. When and why are hands laid on people in your church?

7. Do you think 12:25 is the beginning of the new passage or the conclusion of the preceding passage? Why?

Chapter Five: Address in Asia

Acts 13:4–47

Introduction

i. In the second part of Acts there is an awful lot of travelling! Luke now tells how Paul, always working with others, takes the gospel into the world. The part of Asia Minor visited by 'Team Paul' in this chapter formed the Roman province of Galatia; not long after his visit Paul sent the Epistle to the Galatians to these people.

ii. Paul saw himself as a flexible person (see 1 Corinthians 9:19–23) and this is indeed visible from the way in which he works: he meets very different people and works easily with all of them. But whatever he says, his message is always about Jesus, the risen Lord.

iii. After short sections on Paul's journeys to Cyprus (4–12) and Perge and Antioch (13), this chapter consists of Paul's speech in 'the other Antioch' (14–41) and its effects (42–47).

Background Information

i. Luke does not explain the names of the apostle to the gentiles, Saul, also known as Paul. In 7:58 he was introduced under the Jewish name Saul but during his work outside Israel he obviously carries the Latin name Paul. In Acts 13:9 we simply read that he had two names. As a Roman citizen, born in Tarsus, he probably had both names from childhood and used them according to the situation. From here Luke will consistently call him Paul.

ii. The sermons (speeches) in Acts are shortened renderings of longer speeches. It takes us only a few minutes to read them, while the speakers almost certainly spoke for at least an hour at a time, as can be seen in Acts 20:9. In line with the practice of all ancient historians, Luke has summarised the key points and omitted the repetitions. Acts contains eight 'evangelistic' speeches: three by Paul (chapters 13, 14, 17) and five by Peter (2, 3, 4, 5 and 10). It is striking that only some of them mention God's wrath and judgement, whereas all clearly mention Jesus Christ and his resurrection.

Luke gives much attention to the speech in this chapter, setting it up as a model of how Paul would also speak in other places; as a result, in 14:1 and 21 he only has to say that Paul 'spoke' and 'proclaimed'.

iii. Jews were living everywhere in the Roman Empire, meeting in synagogues. It appears that in Philippi there was no synagogue (16:13). Wherever he comes, Paul begins by addressing the local Jews (cf. Romans 1:16). For this reason, his title 'apostle to the gentiles' seems not quite appropriate here.

iv. At that time many cities were called Antioch, all named after the father of the first Seleucid king. The city where Paul now comes is another ('in Pisidia', verse 14) and smaller city than the large Antioch in Syria from which he had set out (verse 1).

v. Persecution of the followers of Jesus is a theme that occurs throughout Acts; usually the perpetrators are Jews who do not recognise Jesus as their Messiah, but sometimes also gentiles. Paul comments on his suffering under persecution in 2 Corinthians 11:22–12:10.

Explanation of the Text

13:4–5 Seleucia is the port city of Antioch. Cyprus is a logical choice as a destination because Barnabas came from this island (4:36). Salamis and Paphos were the two most important cities on the island, situated at either end of it. John or John Mark (12:12, 25; the former name is Jewish, the latter Roman) is the same person who later wrote the Gospel of Mark (cf. 1 Peter 5:13). Paul often took a younger person as his 'helper', think of Timothy, but the introduction of John Mark here sounds like an afterthought. Acts 15:39 suggests that John Mark also had relatives in Cyprus.

13:6 Bar-Jesus means 'son of Jesus' (cf. Bartimaeus, Mark 10:46). The name Jesus or Joshua was common among Jews. Paul handles this wizard in the tradition of Moses, with a miracle of divine judgment (Exodus 7:11–12; 8:18–19; 9:11, where the word 'magician' or 'sorcerer' is used).

13:7 Sergius Paulus is not known outside the Bible. He is called 'wise' because he is not bothered by the magician.

13:8 There is a spiritual battle.

13:9–11 Because the magician hinders his proclamation, Paul announces a heavy punishment: the man will temporarily be blind. (Luke does not tell when his blindness was healed again; was that after he accepted God?) The punishing sign displays the power of God with the result that the one to whom Paul proclaimed the gospel comes to faith (verse 12). In an environment full of sorcery, Paul must show that his God is the strongest. He calls the sorcerer 'son of the devil' instead of 'son of Jesus'. (So NRSV and ESV; NIV's translation 'child' fails to bring out the allusion to his real name.) In the world of the Middle East 'son' or 'child' often indicates spiritual kinship (e.g. Mark 3:17, Galatians 4:28).

13:12 The conversion of the proconsul will have had a positive effect in his environment.

13:13 The apostles sail from Cyprus to present-day Turkey. They probably landed in Attalia; Perge is situated inland. The reason for Mark's departure is not told, but Paul blamed him for a long time before they were reconciled (15:37–38).

13:14 Luke clearly distinguishes this smaller Antioch from the large Antioch in Syria.

13:15 It was not unusual for guests to be invited to give an address in a synagogue (cf. Luke 4:16–21).

13:16–41 Paul speaks about Jesus' person and his ministry, and about the response expected of the hearers.

13:16 Besides the ethnic Jews, Paul addresses proselytes, people of pagan descent who worshipped God (cf. verses 26, 43).

13:17–22 Paul summarises the history of Israel. By using the word 'our' (verse 17) he identifies with his Jewish hearers. The seven nations (verse 19) come from Deuteronomy 7:1. The word translated here as 'overthrow' also means 'humiliate' or 'subject'.

13:21 Paul, or Saul, was probably called after this king, and he was also from the tribe of Benjamin (Philippians 3:5).

13:22 David is described as the ideal king of Israel with words from Psalm 89:20, 1 Samuel 13:14 and Isaiah 44:28.

13:23–24, 27, 32 Paul jumps from David to Jesus and presents him as the fulfilment of God's promises to his people. He later quotes Psalm 2:7 (in verse 33), Psalm 16:10 (verse 35), Habakkuk 1:5 (verse 41) and Isaiah 49:6 (verse 47). Verse 29 is an allusion to Deuteronomy 21:23 and verse 34 to Isaiah 55:3.

13:26 This is the pivotal thesis of the speech: 'Jewish brothers and sisters, the Scriptures have now been fulfilled because Jesus is the promised Messiah.'

13:27 This is the paradox of the death of Jesus: it was badly intended but used for good by God.

13:29 For 'cross' the Greek text has 'wood' and older NIV versions 'tree'. Paul uses this particular word here and in Galatians 3:13 because of the connection with Deuteronomy 21:22–23.

13:30–37 The resurrection of Jesus is central to Paul's words. It is important that there are eyewitnesses (verse 31).

13:32 To 'raise up' here is to 'give a role'.

13:36–37 Paul explains that Psalm 16 points to Jesus much more than it does to David.

13:38–41 Paul presents the people with the choice: on the one hand Jesus, the forgiveness of sins and justification. On the other he derives a warning from the Greek translation of Habakkuk 1:5, which is sharper than the Hebrew text (verse 41). Just like God's Word could not be ignored under the Old Covenant, so it cannot be now. That the law does not save people is also stated in Galatians 2:16.

13:44 Not only some Jews want to hear about Jesus, but also many gentiles (cf. verse 48). What a great result! On the other hand, most Jews reject the gospel and respond in a hostile way (verse 45, cf. 50). This will happen to Paul more often, see e.g. Acts 17:5–7, 13; 18:5–6; 19:9; 20:3).

13:47 The apostles apply the messianic prophecy of Isaiah 49:6 to their own work as messengers of the Messiah. The work of Christ is not only for the Jews but also for the gentiles.

Application

1. Paul never travelled alone. He was much more a member of a team than the common expression 'the missionary travels of Paul' suggests. In all ages, solo-

ministries have a greater risk of going off the rails than team-ministries.

2. We all have been given different gifts, but they can and should be developed.

3. While in his letters Paul often emphasizes the crucifixion of the Lord Jesus, Luke has especially remembered that Paul spoke of the resurrection of the Lord. We should do justice to both aspects of what Christ has done for us.

4. Paul quotes many verses from the Old Testament to support his preaching. In his time there were no written Gospels yet from which he could quote. How we tell people about Jesus should certainly depend on the kind of persons to whom we are speaking.

For Thought and Discussion

1. Think about how you share the gospel, if you do so at all. Do you identify with the person to whom you are talking, like Paul did?

2. Which verses or passages from the Old Testament would *you* use to explain who Jesus is? And which verses from the New Testament make this most clear in your opinion?

3. What does Paul say about the cross here and what about the resurrection? How many words does he use for each of these?

4. When the gospel is being proclaimed, should the wrath of God always be mentioned?

5. The cross is probably the most common Christian symbol. How could we symbolise the resurrection?

Chapter Six: Prisoner in Europe

Acts 16

Introduction

i. Acts 16 follows immediately after 15:36–41, which reports that Paul has parted company with Barnabas because of a dispute which Luke describes in an impartial way. Paul has chosen Silas as his new co-worker and together they travel among the existing congregations in present-day Turkey. Yet when they reach unreached territories, the Holy Spirit prevents them from preaching the gospel. In the end they come to the sea that separates them from Europe.

ii. The events in the second half of the chapter take place in Europe, in the city of Philippi. This section is full of spectacular elements: a mob (19–22), an assault and imprisonment (23), an earthquake (26) and repentance (32–33). Paul's later letter to the Philippians shows that he had managed to build a long, deep relationship with the congregation which he had founded in this city against this backdrop.

Background Information

i. This chapter contains the first passage that Luke writes in the we-form (first person plural). That is to say, from verse 10 onwards he does not use 'he' or 'they' but 'we' to tell his story. This change shows that Luke himself was likely present at the events he narrates: he was an eyewitness! Apparently he joined

'Team Paul' at Troas, but it is strange and unusual that he fails to introduce himself to us as readers. The parts of Acts written in this we-form are 16:10–17; 20:5–15; 21:1–18 and 27:1–28:16.

ii. Timothy becomes Paul's assistant and friend (see e.g. 17:14–15; 18:5; 19:22; Romans 16:21) and the co-author of various letters. Paul also addressed two letters to him.

iii. Verses 6–8 do not provide enough details to allow us to reconstruct Paul's itinerary. In any case he travels from east to west through Turkey. The province of Asia (verse 6) is a smaller part of Asia Minor or present-day Turkey. The port of Troas (verse 8) was strategically situated on the route between Turkey (Asia Minor) and Greece. Samothrace (verse 11) is near a high mountain that formed a striking beacon for sailors. Neapolis was the name of the port of Philippi. The city itself is called a colony, which is a settlement of Roman citizens; this explains why so few Jews lived in the city that there was not even a synagogue.

iv. The ancient Greeks already distinguished between the continents of Asia, Africa and Europe. Paul and Luke must have been aware of this boundary.

Explanation of the Text

16:1–2 Paul had previously visited these cities, see 14:6.

16:3 Paul had a consistent policy: believers with a pagan background did not need to be circumcised (see Acts 21:21 and his Letter to the Galatians, especially 2:3) – but Jewish believers had to be circumcised (cf. 1 Corinthians 9:19–22). Paul always urged Jewish Christians to comply with the law of Moses, and so – as the son of a Jewish woman – Timothy ought to be circumcised. It was possibly Timothy's father who had prevented his circumcision as a baby.

Timothy always remains in the shadow of Paul, but Paul's two letters to him show that he was a good and trusted friend for Paul. He was the co-author of wise letters such as 2 Corinthians – and who knows how big his share in writing it really was?

16:4–5 The decision taken by the council in Jerusalem, namely that the Christians from the gentiles do not need to keep the whole law (Acts 15), has a positive impact on the existing congregations in Asia Minor. Allegiance to Jesus was now of course more attractive to male outsiders.

16:6–8 After completing his reporting on the council's decisions, Paul is free to make his own plans. Here he starts a new journey, but he and his travelling companions do not know the route in advance. They are dependent on God's guidance. Whereas the Holy Spirit usually provides 'positive' guidance, here he merely prevents Paul from doing the obvious. This 'negative' approach does not occur anywhere else in Acts. The best explanation is that the Spirit is preparing Paul to travel to Macedonia while Paul himself has not thought of this option.

In these verses the guidance comes from the Holy Spirit (see also 13:2; 15:28; 21:4), but elsewhere in Acts God (14:27; 18:21) and Jesus (13:47; 14:3–4) are named as source of guidance. Acts 20:3 states that Paul himself made a plan. These things do not contradict each other but work together.

16:9 From the port of Troas one could sail in all directions. Paul now experiences positive guidance by the Spirit: he has a dream about a person asking for help. Typically, the apostle interprets 'help' to mean the preaching of the gospel. After the previous opposition from the Spirit Paul does not need any further guidance.

Luke emphatically uses the name Macedonia three times in a few sentences: there, in that part of Europe, the gospel must be preached.

16:10 Paul obeys immediately, seeking a suitable cargo ship. Of course, there were no scheduled ferry services in that era. On the sudden use of 'we', see the 'Background Information' for this chapter (above).

16:11 The journey is very smooth.

16:12 A colony is a place where veterans of the Roman army lived, and which therefore had autonomy.

16:13 Apparently there is no synagogue in the city itself, and Paul meets only women, which suggests that there were very few Jews in Philippi.

16:14–15 Lydia is one of the prominent female characters in Acts. The name Lydia is possibly a nickname, meaning 'the Lydian', 'the lady from the country of Lydia'. Her hometown of Thyatira is in Lydia, present-day Turkey. In Thyatira as well as in Philippi and Thessalonica inscriptions have been found about the craft of dyeing purple. Lydia's house was apparently large enough to accommodate the complete Team Paul.

16:16–18 We do not know how many weeks later this event happens. A slave girl who is being abused as a fairground attraction meets Paul. The Old Testament is very critical about predicting the future so Paul is apprehensive.

The name of Jesus Christ (verse 18) is stronger than the evil power. Yet although Paul performs a mighty miracle in the name of Jesus, no one comes to faith because he has been placed in a bad light. It is striking that the evil spirit knows that Paul's message is a positive one (verse 17).

16:19–21 This time it is not the Jews who denounce Paul with the authorities. Luke gives an ironic view of the anti-Jewish feelings of the Roman settlers, who were proud of their status as Romans. What really matters to them is the money, but they talk about the disruption of public order. The leaders of the city are first identified as 'authorities', then more precisely as 'magistrates'.

16:22–24 Without any opportunity to defend themselves, Paul and Silas are tortured and secured. The Roman government does not show a very civilised face. And Paul does not speak up about his

Roman citizenship at this point (though he does later, see verse 37), but Luke does not say why.

16:25 This familiar verse is an encouragement for many believers in difficult circumstances. God is there, even in that dungeon. And you can praise him under all circumstances.

16:26 This earthquake is a miracle because there is great material damage, but no-one is injured. Elsewhere in the city life continues as normal, see for example verse 35.

16:27 There is no rational explanation for this suicide attempt, because the escape of any prisoners would not be the fault of the jailor. It seems sheer panic.

16:28 Luke does not tell us how Paul knows this.

16:30–31 The concise report of the events leaves the question open, of what this man needed to be saved. Had Paul spoken about the judgement of God? In the context it is more likely that the man had used the term 'save' in view of his own difficult situation, upon which Paul replied to him using his own expression. Whether or not the man was aware of his situation before God we do not know.

16:32–34 What a contrast with the reaction of the other Philippians!

16:35–36 The city magistrates want to let Paul off with a (severe!) warning.

16:37–38 Of course Paul was not ethnically a Roman, but he was a Roman citizen (21:39; 22:25). This status guaranteed legal protection against torture. The magistrates faced punishment by the Roman proconsul because they had tortured a citizen.

16:39 Paul and Silas obviously claim their rights, not just in their own interest, but for the sake of the believers in the city: it must be made publicly clear that no member of the new religious movement has committed any crime.

16:40 Apparently Luke stays behind in Philippi, because the narrative form changes from 'we' to 'they'.

Application

1. The Macedonian man does not dream of Paul. People do not often ask us questions about our faith. Yet we believe that we have a message for the world. We know the way. That is not a hollow pretension, it is the certainty of faith.

2. Paul takes the request of the Macedonian man as a as a call for him to preach the gospel. You can only do so when you are convinced that the gospel is relevant, when you are sure that Jesus is indeed the answer to the need of every person.

3. The world needs help. It needs food, water, medical care, peace. What motivates us is the gospel, God's love for people. On this basis we can also provide practical assistance.

Although in our own situation we are unlikely to meet a spirit which predicts the future, we have to take the story seriously.

For Thought and Discussion

1. Do you experience God's guidance in your life? If so, how? If not, do you miss it?

2. 'Come over and help us.' Is it logical to bring the gospel in response to this call?

3. What do you think of this old comparison: passing on the good news about Jesus is like a beggar who knows where there is bread, telling another beggar?

4. Christians from the gentiles need not keep the law and, for example, do not need to be circumcised. Modern Christians sometimes appear to live as if no law applies to them at all. Do you know examples of this attitude? What do you think of it?

5. Check out which letters Timothy wrote together with Paul.

Chapter Seven: Three Greek Cities

Acts 17

Introduction

i. This chapter tells the adventures of Paul in three different cities; the headings in the NIV clearly indicate the parts of the chapter. Paul's stay in the smaller Berea is an interlude between two major cities.

ii. Paul had probably wanted to stay in Thessalonica for a long time, but circumstances soon propelled him to Athens. Here he proclaims the gospel to Jews and ordinary people (verse 17), but also to the city elite. In addressing the latter group, he is mindful of what they are likely to understand. When speaking to Jews he makes much use of the Old Testament and talks about the history of Israel – but now he takes a rather different approach because these gentiles do not know the Scriptures. Instead he finds a connecting point between the altar for the unknown god and the belief in a creator. His speech in Athens is the only one of its kind in Acts. Paul speaks respectfully, but his appeal is not an attempt at a dialogue between equals.

Background Information

i. Thessalonica was the capital of the Roman province of Macedonia, that is, the northern half of Greece. Shortly after his stay in Thessalonica Paul had already written a letter to the congregation which had formed, and within a year a second letter. These letters were primarily aimed at young Christians.

ii. Athens had once been a very important city, but in Paul's time it was past its zenith. Yet it was still a centre of philosophy, that is, thinking about life. Luke is very ironic about this in verse 21. In addition, the people were very religious; in an attempt not to offend any deity there was even an altar for one whom they might have overlooked (verse 23). Paul's work in this city only has limited results.

iii. Luke knows much about the cities where Paul visits and about the philosophers whom he meets in Athens. Verse 18 mentions two groups: Stoics believed that just about everything in the world was divine. Paul ties in with their faith in the unity of humankind and in the kinship between God and humans (verses 26–27). Epicureans believed that humans did not need to seek God because probably no God existed. Paul joins their opposition to superstition (verse 24).

Explanation of the Text

17:1 Amphipolis and Apollonia were known as staging points on the road from Philippi to Thessalonica. Luke's wording suggests that they probably did not have a synagogue.

17:2–3 We observe the by now fixed pattern: conversation with the Jews – opening up the Scriptures – Jesus – cross and resurrection. The Greek word for 'to reason' is related to our word dialogue:

Paul enters into a conversation about the Scriptures, see also 17:17; 18:4, 19; 19:8, 9.

17:4 More Greeks than Jews come to faith; Luke emphatically mentions the upper-class women (cf. verse 12). 'Quite a few' (literally 'not a few', see NRSV) is Luke's favourite way of saying 'many'.

17:5 The Jews are jealous because Paul steals their sheep: the gentiles who now accept Jesus were God-fearing people who were already close to Judaism. Jason, probably Paul's host, is not introduced to us. This name was very common and it is therefore uncertain whether Romans 16:21 refers to the same person.

17:6 Possibly the people in Thessalonica had heard what had happened in Philippi, but in any case, the accusation is heavily exaggerated. 'City officials' is the translation of a rare Greek word (*politarches*). It used to be thought that Luke had made up this word, but an inscription found in Thessalonica does contain the term.

17:7 This part of the accusation is correct, so Paul was well understood. If Jesus is the only King and Lord, the Emperor cannot also be. Some imperial decrees stipulated that it was illegal to predict a change of government.

17:9 The bail is probably intended to guarantee that Paul will leave the city; and so his departure is inevitable. In 1 Thessalonians 2:17–18 he looks back at his sudden departure with regret.

17:10–14 In Berea, Paul acts in his well-known way. His Jewish interlocutors are more open and so there is more fruit. The eagerness of the Bereans is an example for us. It is unclear why Silas and Timothy are not at risk from the attack on Paul. For the third time Paul is forced out of a European city.

17:16 Paul simply resents the idols of Athens. Nowhere else in the Bible is an evangelist so negative about a place as Paul is here.

17:17 Paul calms down quickly. From the outset he divides his attention between the Jews and Greeks.

17:18 'Babbler' is a rude word from the Athenian street language. The word resurrection (Greek: *anastasis*) is misunderstood as a reference to a goddess named Anastasia.

17:19, 22 The Areopagus or Hill of Mars overlooks the city's central market square. Luke seems to use the name here as a reference to the court which met on this site. Dionysius (verse 34) was a member of this court. It is unclear whether Paul is being heard formally or whether this is an informal conversation.

17:21 This comment is both sarcastic and true.

17:22–31 Paul spends most of his speech making connections with his audience. It is not until the final two verses (30–31) that he comes to the core of the gospel. In the original Greek various rhetorical sound effects are apparent, which would have made the speech extra attractive.

17:22–23 The benevolent introduction of the speech. The altar is also mentioned by other writers. Paul does not pronounce a judgement on it, he does not approve of it either, but he makes good use of it. Verse 23 can also, more literally, be translated 'What therefore you worship as unknown [or: without understanding it], this I proclaim to you' (NRSV).

17:24–25 Paul's first point is that God is Lord over all the world. As he was speaking these words, Paul could point at the temples which surrounded him. His criticism resembles that of Stephen and the prophets (Acts 7:48–50).

17:26–27 The second point is that God is the creator, and that humankind needs him.

17:28–29 Paul makes his third point, that God and humanity are related, by quoting two Greek writers: first the Cretan Epimenides and then the Stoic Aratus. This shows how well he understands his audience. He may have read these books himself but it is more likely that he had heard about them.

17:30–31 The conclusion of the speech. Paul ends up with the Lord Jesus and gives him all the glory. In the Old Testament it is God who will judge the world. Paul's words imply that he associates Jesus closely with the Father, but he does not say this explicitly, because that would make matters too complicated for his hearers. The way in which he mentions judgement resembles Peter's words in 10:42: Jesus is the judge who will in the future judge the inhabited world. The Greeks did not know the concept of a final judgement, so that Paul would have much to explain afterwards. He concludes, however, with a reference to the resurrection of the dead. This sounded just as absurd in the ears of his Greek audience. The reference to the resurrection implies that Paul also mentioned the death of the Lord.

17:32–34 The reactions are quite diverse. Luke knows the names of a few converts, but the majority politely keep their distance. 'Areopagite' means a member of the court that met there.

Application

1. Paul has a different conception of culture than the Athenians and the Greeks in general. Athens was a beautiful city filled with memories of a glorious past, but Paul sees only the disgusting side of its idolatry and reacts vigorously. Many contemporary Christians are hardly upset by idols, because we are no longer sensitive (= vulnerable) to the forces that were at work behind them. I think that Paul's reaction was correct in his time, but that we do not have to become alarmed as well.

2. Although Paul initially seeks a connexion with his hearers, at the end of his speech he is quite confrontational. This approach is a good example for us: start the conversation about faith where your interlocutor is, build a bridge, but do not unduly dilute the message.

3. Paul knows his audience and responds to their thoughts and beliefs. For us, this approach means that

we need to get under the skin of the person facing us with their specific ideas. In our era of individualism we cannot assume that we know what the person opposite us thinks or feels.

For Thought and Discussion

1. If Jesus is Lord, what is the status and place of other rulers (verse 7)? What does this mean in practice?

2. Compare the speeches in Acts 3, 13 and 17 with each other. How does the speaker accommodate to his audience in each case?

3. Which parts of the Old Testament does Paul use in verses 24–31?

4. Do the people around you ridicule the resurrection from the dead in the same way as the Greeks? Or do they believe in so many supernatural things that this can easily be added to the list? Why is it important that you know this?

5. Have you ever experienced the response of a Christian from another part of the world to an idol or something similar? How did you react?

6. What is your view of the many representations of Buddha that are for sale in our shops? Are there demonic powers behind these things? If you have them into your home, what are you communicating to any visitors?

7. Paul accepts certain ideas of the Athenians but disagrees with other ones. In our time for many, especially young black and Asian British men, Islam is

an attractive alternative to Christianity. Which elements of Islam can you accept and which do you reject?

Chapter Eight: Acquittal in Corinth

Acts 18:1–23

Introduction

Up to now we have mainly seen Paul travelling round as messenger of the gospel. This now changes, as he is going to spend almost two years in one congregation, the one in Corinth. As usual he first approaches the Jewish population (verses 4–6), then the gentiles (7–11). He is acquitted by the highest judge (12–17) and departs from the city (18–23).

Background to Verses 1–3

i. The commercial port city of Corinth was strategically located on a junction of roads and sailing routes, so that people came there from all over the Roman world. How seriously Paul took his work here is evident from the fact that he wrote no fewer than four letters to the church in this city. In addition to the two letters we have in the Bible, he refers to other letters in 1 Corinthians 5:9 and 2 Corinthians 2:9, but these letters have not been preserved.

ii. The Roman historian Suetonius tells that the Emperor Claudius (ruled AD 41–54) expelled the Jews from Rome in the year 49 because they had internal disagreements over a certain Chrestus, in whom we recognise Christ (Greek *Christos*). As Jewish believers in Christ, Priscilla and Aquila also had to leave Rome. After the death of Claudius his edict was no longer in force and Romans 16:3 shows us that Priscilla and Aquila were again living in Rome when Paul wrote Romans in about the year AD 57.

iii. Paul's co-workers Aquila and Priscilla are clearly formidable believers in their own right. Note that they have the stature to teach the learned Apollos (18:24–26). Remarkably, Luke mentions the woman, Priscilla, before her husband in 18:18 and 26. But when you consult 18:26 in the King James Version you see Aquila mentioned first, because medieval scribes changed the Greek text to reflect what they found acceptable. Newer translations are based on better Greek manuscripts.

Background to Verses 8 and 17

In verse 8 the leader of the synagogue in Corinth is called Crispus, but in verse 17 Sosthenes. The church father John Chrysostom already believed that these names indicate the same person. The meanings of the names support this explanation: Crispus means vibrating, unstable; not a good name for a Christian. The meaning of the name Sosthenes, on the other hand, is positive: something like 'powerful saviour', 'safe in power'. As a result of his conversion Mr. Unstable had become Mr. Stable in Strength. Later he helped Paul to write 1 Corinthians (1:1). It is understandable that the Jews who do not believe in Jesus vent their frustrations on him (verse 17), because he would have been a major mainstay of Paul in the city.

Background to Verses 12–17

i. Achaia was the Roman province of which Corinth was the capital; it covered the southern part of Greece.

ii. Junius Annaeus Gallio, born in Cordoba, Spain, was consul (mayor) of the city of Rome in the year AD 56, but in AD 65 the mad Emperor Nero forced him to commit suicide. An inscription from Greece makes mention of him as proconsul of Achaia. Proconsuls served for only one year, from July to June, and this inscription shows that Gallio ruled Achaia between 1 July AD 51 and 30 June AD 52. With the help of this information we can date Paul's stay in Corinth rather exactly! And from this fixed point Paul's whole life is dated, from his conversion around the year 35 until his arrival in Rome in 60. He probably died around the year 67.

iii. The proconsul was the highest judge in affairs of religion and public order in his province (cf. 19:38).

Explanation of the Text

18:1–2 Paul meets a Jewish couple who have just arrived in the city from Italy. They had left Rome on the orders of the Emperor Claudius, see above. Although Luke does not say so explicitly, they are clearly followers of Jesus and their companionship is therefore an encouragement for Paul.

18:3 Paul was a manual worker by profession (cf. 1 Corinthians 4:12, 2 Thessalonians 3:8). Many people from the region of Tarsus (cf. 21:39) were tentmakers.

Tents were sometimes made of goats' hair but mostly of leather.

18:4 As always Paul begins his ministry with the Jews. Luke's choice of words suggests that he was discussing the Scriptures with them.

18:5 Paul's friends had been in Berea and Thessalonica (cf. 17:14); their arrival is a further encouragement for Paul. From Corinth Paul wrote the two letters to the Thessalonians as soon as Silas and Timothy arrived.

The fact that Paul can now fully commit himself to proclamation and teaching, without having to work, suggests that Silas and Timothy had brought some financial support with them.

18:6–7 Paul's extra activity causes resistance. The abuse of the Jews makes working in the synagogue impossible for Paul. The shaking out of clothes or feet is a symbolic act that signifies disconnection from a community (Nehemiah 5:13; Matthew 10:14; Acts 13:51).

18:9–10 Why is Paul given this vision? Probably because he expected an attack from the Jews in Corinth, similar to the ones he had suffered in other places (9:23–25, 29; 13:50; 14:5–6, 19; 17:5–6). So Jesus encourages his servant. 'I have many people in this city' suggests that Jesus wants to use Paul to reach these people with the gospel; this implies that Paul will neither be killed nor chased out of the city.

18:11 As result of the vision Paul finds the courage to stay in Corinth for a long period of time. This will have led to considerable growth of the congregation. See also verse 8.

18:12 The Jews try to benefit from the arrival of a new, inexperienced proconsul. From the Greek text it is unclear whether the Jews used violence or whether Paul appeared voluntarily before this judge.

18:13–14a Judaism was a recognised religion, and Jews had certain freedoms in the Roman Empire. But the Jews accuse Paul of not being a good Jew, which would yet place him outside the law. The very short report of the court proceedings suggests that Gallio was not very interested in the case. He even prevents Paul from speaking and is not open to the word of God.

18:14b–15 Gallio declares the indictment against Paul inadmissible. According to him, it is a problem of the Jews among themselves. Nothing has happened that would require a Roman legal verdict.

18:16–17 The Jews vent their disappointment and anger at Sosthenes. Thus Sosthenes must suffer for the discharge of Paul. It is downright immoral that Gallio allows this innocent man to be beaten in his presence.

18:18a The NRSV is correct to render 'a considerable time'. It is striking that Priscilla is often mentioned before her husband Aquila, and it suggests that she had a more important position than he. See the Background Information above. Luke does not tell us why Paul departs; it almost seems as if he is going on leave to Antioch.

18:18b Jews made vows as a thanksgiving for blessings received or as a request for divine help for the future. Here we probably have to do with the former, but Luke does not give any details. It is once again evident that in many respects Paul lived as a Jew; this is not contrary to his faith in Jesus, see 1 Corinthians 9:20. Cenchreae was one of the seaports connected to Corinth.

18:18–22 After eighteen months in Corinth the three of them depart for Ephesus. There Priscilla and Aquila stay behind, while Paul quickly travels on to Jerusalem and subsequently to his home church in Antioch. He probably wanted to be in Jerusalem for Easter. Paul's return to Ephesus, in response to the request of the local Jews (verse 20), is reported in Acts 19.

18:22–23 Luke summarises many miles in a few words. Caesarea was virtually the only port city in Israel. Paul only briefly visits the 'mother church' in Jerusalem – the name of the city has been added by the translators of the latest NIV because Luke only mentions 'the congregation' (Greek *ekklesia*).

Paul spends more time in his home church in Antioch. According to verse 18, that was also his destination ('Syria'). It seems that he feels more at home in this multicultural community than in the church in Jerusalem. Then he journeys over land across Asia Minor to Ephesus on the west coast. It is striking that en route he makes no attempt to establish any new congregations but merely supports the existing ones.

This suggests that these churches themselves were able to pass the gospel on while Paul's commitment was to Ephesus.

Application

1. The legal importance of Gallio's verdict is enormous but easily overlooked. He concludes that the accusation against Paul is inadmissible. The Romans always stepped in whenever there were religious troubles if they thought that the interest of the state demanded this. Thus Paul had only recently been removed from Philippi (Acts 16:39) and Claudius had banished the Jews from Rome (18:2). Yet here in Corinth Gallio recognises the Christian faith on behalf of Rome as not in any way a danger to the state, because it is part of Judaism, a permitted religion. This issue was so important for Luke and his readers that he continues to repeat it in the final chapters of Acts: Paul is innocent, the Christian faith is harmless to the state. May this conclusion also reach present-day governments which are persecuting Christians!

2. Paul does not continually travel round, but settles for a long time in a strategic town. Verses 22–23 also point out that he was working according to a plan. This discovery should guide us when we think about how we can effectively pass on the gospel.

For Thought and Discussion

1. Do you find the historical information in this chapter interesting? If so, can you find some more on

the internet? (Tip: A search by 'Gallio inscription' brings up some stunning pictures.)

2. A preacher (pastor) who also earns money by working with his hands – is that acceptable or desirable? Do you know the concept of a 'tentmaker' in mission at home and overseas?

3. 'Do not be afraid' (verse 9): where else in the Bible do you encounter this encouragement?

4. If you could adopt a (new) Christian name, like Crispus, how would you want to be called and why?

5. What reasons do national governments have to consider the Christian faith as a threat to the state? Can you respond to these reasons?

6. Can you explain why Paul's faith in Jesus is not contrary to the Jewish faith?

7. Could it be better to settle down as an evangelist in a particular town or village than always to be on the move?

Chapter Nine: Exploits in Ephesus

Acts 19:1, 8–40

Introduction

i. Here we see a familiar pattern: where the light breaks through, the resistance of the darkness also increases. This same phenomenon had been visible during the earthly ministry of Jesus.

ii. Our section consists of two general overviews of Paul's work in Ephesus (verses 8–12, 18–20) and two confrontations with opposition: by Jews (13–17) and by gentiles (23–40). The verses 21–22 are a kind of interim conclusion. Luke does not describe the content of Paul's preaching because he has already done so in previous chapters.

iii. Luke probably has several reasons for including the long scene in the theatre:

a). He has reported the resistance from the side of the Jews previously and now he wants to balance the books: gentiles also oppose the gospel.

b). He can show that the resistance to the gospel is based on a mixture of jealousy, greed for money and misplaced nationalism.

c). To enforce the message of the previous chapter, he makes it clear that a reasonable person like the city clerk sees no harm in the work of Paul. The gospel is no threat to the state. For Luke's first readers, believers who lived in the Roman Empire, this was an important statement.

iv. Apart from this, Luke is remarkably restrained in his reporting; Paul himself writes much more openly about huge difficulties he encountered in Ephesus, see 1 Corinthians 15:32 and 2 Corinthians 1:8–10.

Background Information

i. We often refer to the three 'missionary journeys' of Paul, but that is a modern construction, not something Luke mentions. Although during his first 'journey' Paul did not find peace in Asia Minor, he later lived in the large port cities of Corinth and Ephesus for years. Both cities were strategically located and served as hubs from where Team Paul worked in the surrounding areas (19:10, 26). Verses 22 and 29 mention some of Paul's co-workers. Epaphras is likely to be the one who founded the congregations in Colossae and Laodicea, where Paul himself did not go (Colossians 1:6–7).

ii. Ephesus was one of the largest cities in the Roman Empire, the largest city in Asia Minor (= Asia, verse 10) and a strategic port. No wonder Paul was going to live here! Among other things, he wrote 1 Corinthians here in the year 55.

iii. The temple of the goddess Artemis (or Diana) in Ephesus was one of the largest and most beautiful buildings in the world and was regarded as one of the Seven Wonders of the World. It was a centre of religion and commerce because people took their money there. A legend had it that the large statue of the goddess had fallen from heaven in a ready-made form (verse 35). The large theatre in which the population gathered still exists; it was a solid piece of Roman architecture.

iv. In verses 9 and 23 the followers of Jesus are again referred to as 'The Way', cf. 9:2; 18:25–26; 22:4; 24:14, 22.

Explanation of the Text

19:1 Luke had interrupted his record of Paul's journey after 18:23 and now picks up the thread. Paul arrives in the coastal town of Ephesus from the mountainous area.

19:8–9 After reporting an incident at the beginning of Paul's ministry (verses 2–7), Luke gives an overview of Paul's work at Ephesus. The pattern is familiar: first he goes to the Jews – some Jews believe in Jesus – break with the Jews in the synagogue – the Christians come together separately and focus on proclamation to the gentiles. On the kingdom of God, see at 1:3.

A 'lecture hall' or 'school' (KJV) was a public building. Paul is holding his meetings in an accessible place! Almost certainly he is combining this work with his profession of tentmaker (cf. 18:3).

19:10 Paul works even longer in Ephesus than in Corinth. From the city multiple trade routes went into the interior parts of Asia Minor, and Paul likely sent his co-workers in all directions.

19:11–12 Luke does not report the many miracles performed by Paul in detail. It is probably because Ephesus had a reputation as a city of magic and because the inhabitants were in the grip of superstitions, that God proves his power here. Like Paul's work in Athens this is a case of responding to the local situation. Hence what is happening here is probably not an example for all times.

19:13–14 The Jews in Asia Minor were also known as superstitious, but there are virtually no stories about real miracles among Jews from the time after the Old Testament. It seems that the people who are mentioned here want to ride on the wave of Paul's success. They know that they themselves have no authority over evil spirits, but that Jesus does. 'Chief priest' is probably the title which Sceva had awarded to himself; Jewish priests only officiated in the temple in Jerusalem.

19:15–16 This evil spirit has considerable power. On what evil spirits know, see Luke 4:34, 41; 8:28. We may assume that Jesus is stronger, for although Luke does not state this, it is implied in verse 17.

19:17, 20 As a result of all things that take place a strong local church comes into being (verse 20) with a formidable reputation (17).

19:19 A drachma or silver coin was a day's wages. Scrolls – the form books took in those days, before the invention of books with covers and pages – were hand-written and consequently very costly.

19:21–23 Paul thinks ahead and plans a tour through Greece – but just before his departure another incident takes place. The words 'in the Spirit' (see NIV footnote) are actually in the Greek text. They can be taken as 'in the (Holy) Spirit' (see NRSV and ESV) or 'in his own spirit' (see KJV). These possibilities do not exclude each other. In his letters Paul reports that during this period he was carrying out a collection for the church in Jerusalem (Romans 15:25–33; 1 Corinthians 16:1–3) but Luke only hints at this effort in Acts 24:17.

19:24 Artisans made small replicas of the famous temple. We know that the craftsmen in Asia were united in guilds.

19:25 Demetrius addresses his guild. He first mentions the economic importance of the trade, only secondarily its religious importance.

19:26 Of course Paul is not the only person who knows that idols are merely lifeless statues; by way of illustration you can read Isaiah 45:14–25.

19:27 Indeed Ephesus later became a major city for early Christianity, until the coming of Islam in the seventh century. The proud temple of Artemis was destroyed in AD 262, which must have been a massive blow to the worship of the goddess. For centuries afterwards no-one even knew where the temple had been situated!

19:28 Religious fanaticism has always existed – and it is always dangerous.

19:29. Theatres doubled up as meeting places for the residents.

19:31 For 'officials of the province' Luke uses the appropriate word 'Asiarch' (as in ESV), that is, ruler over Asia. Again it is evident that Paul has many contacts in the upper circles (see e.g. 13:7–12).

19:32–34 First Luke supplies some humorous commentary, but then he reveals the antisemitism among the people. The situation with the whipped-up crowd is in fact life-threatening and Paul's advisors were quite right in telling him to stay away (verses 30–31). The Jew Alexander is literally pushed forward by the other Jews as their representative, so that they can dissociate themselves from Paul, but the gentiles do not want to listen to him.

19:35 The transition is better translated in the NRSV: *'But* when the town clerk had quietened the crowd, he said…' This city clerk (NIV) was not a humble civil servant but 'the most important native official of the provincial capital, [who] was in close touch with the Roman authorities, who would hold him responsible for the riotous assembly' (F.F. Bruce).[1] The main translations give the wrong impression, although the Living Bible has 'the mayor'.

---

[1] *The Acts of the Apostles. The Greek Text with Introduction and Commentary* (London: Tyndale Press, 1951), 367.

'Guardian of the temple' was an honorary title which the Romans granted to important cities. According to local tradition the statue of Artemis had fallen upon the earth as a meteorite.

19:36–40 The sensible leader of the city manages to convince the crowd that they should seek justice somewhere else. He needs a lot of words! Verses 38–39 constitute an appeal to the Roman legal order, which was fully accepted in Asia Minor where the Romans were not seen as an occupying power.

19:40 The Romans had given Ephesus much freedom, but a riot would provoke their intervention. However, the dangerous situation peters out like a candle.

Application

1. The work of Paul bore much fruit: Ephesus became the centre of the church in Asia Minor and remained so for centuries. But this accomplishment came at a cost to the apostle. It is not uncommon that God's servants need to invest much of themselves into their work.

2. In our time 'economic interests' are also extremely important. They often confront followers of Jesus with hard choices: To work on Sundays? Use any means to make a profit? Can I harmonise what my boss wants me to do with my principles?

3. This chapter reveals a tension between the apparent power of some evil spirits (verses 15–16) and the knowledge that idols are merely images. Luke shows

that there is a spiritual reality behind the material reality.

4. Acts shows the believers come together in all sorts of places and at all kinds of times; Luke in no way conveys a fixed pattern for the meetings of The Way. We might like to know more about the transition from Sabbath to Sunday, for example, but apparently this issue is not important.

For Thought and Discussion

1. Above I used the words 'a mixture of jealousy, greed for money and misplaced nationalism' (p. 74). Do these terms do justice to the story?

2. How would you explain to a dictator that the gospel does not threaten the security of the state?

3. What would be a more effective mode of evangelism and church planting: travelling round or settling down? Discuss the advantages and disadvantages of both.

4. Does it bother you that Paul had many contacts among the rich and famous? Why (not)?

5. How much prosperity and security are you willing to surrender for the service of God?

6. Do you have any books (DVDs etc.) that it would be better to burn?

Chapter Ten: Free to Proclaim Jesus in Rome

Acts 28:11–31

Introduction

i. The Book of Acts has an open end. The reader of chapters 21–26 is waiting for the outcome of the trial against Paul before the Emperor. Was he released, as he deserved, or sentenced? And what else happened? Did Paul indeed travel to Spain, as he hoped to do (Romans 15:22–24)? Luke's first readers will have known the answers to these questions, for Luke wrote shortly after the events, and he deliberately omits them. He does not even tell us about Paul's meetings with the Christians in Rome, to whom he had written a long letter, but he directs our attention towards Paul's contacts with the Jews – and more generally towards the proclamation of the gospel in the capital of the known world.

ii. This passage consists of travel information (verses 11–15), Paul's meetings with the Jews (16–29) and concluding remarks (30–31).

Background Information

i. Paul had been arrested in Jerusalem (Acts 21–22) and had subsequently spent two years in prison in Caesarea (23–26, especially 24:27). Now he is being brought to Rome as a prisoner in order to stand trial before the Emperor himself (26:32, 27:1).

The events described in this chapter probably took place in the year AD 60, and verse 30 brings us up to the year 62. (The Epistle to the Romans dates from about the year 55.)

ii. This passage is again in the we-form (see on Acts 16), so Luke is with Paul. After a dramatic shipwreck (chapter 27) and wintering on Malta (28:1–10), they are now reaching their destination.

iii. The contact between Paul and the Jews in Rome shows that at this time the followers of The Way were still seen as a Jewish sect by all parties (verse 22). The separation between Jews and Christians came only later and took place gradually.

iv. Acts has an open end and much has been written about the reasons for this. Experts used to think that Luke wanted to write a third book or that he had died prematurely. We now realise that he consciously left the end open.

In a way Acts is of course complete: a) Luke has placed references to the kingdom of God at the beginning and the end, so that they frame the story, see 1:3, 6 and 28:23, 31. b) The gospel of Jesus has now arrived in the heart of the civilised world. c) Attentive readers know that Paul is innocent, because it has been made clear in chapters 23–26 and it was confirmed when the viper on Malta did not harm him (28:3–6).

v. We have no reliable information about what happened to Paul later in life; there are only later stories and legends.

vi. In response to the persistent unbelief of the Jews, in verses 25–27 Paul quotes from Isaiah 6. Luke has reported that many Jews have come to faith in Jesus, but this time they are few (verse 24). Paul announces judgement upon his hearers and leaves them to their destiny. Isaiah 6 was also cited by Jesus (Matthew 13:14–15) and by John the Evangelist (John 12:37–42). This passage clearly states that whoever refuses to accept the preaching of the word of God will suffer the consequences of this. The Book of Acts does not often confront us with these consequences, because Luke tells more about the positive results of the evangelism than about its rejection.

Explanation of the Text

28:11 Egypt supplied much grain to Rome, which was carried from Alexandria across the Mediterranean Sea by ship, cf. 27:6. However, during the winter it was too dangerous to sail, cf. 27:9, 12.

28:12–13 Syracuse is in Sicily; Regium and Puteoli are in mainland Italy.

28:14–15 Both in the small Puteoli and in Rome there are already Christians before the arrival of Paul. Their presence is an encouragement to him and he is allowed to interrupt his journey, although he is still a prisoner of course.

28:16 As a Roman citizen Paul is presumed innocent until his trial takes place. The Romans here show themselves in a positive light by giving him great freedom.

28:17a Still Paul focuses first on the Jewish inhabitants of the place where he is located (cf. Romans 1:16). Even though he is in Rome as a prisoner he invites them to his place after only three days in town.

28:17b-19 Paul tells the Jews things which the readers of Acts already know from Acts 21–26.

28:20 Paul comes to the point. The expression 'the hope of Israel' (cf. 24:15) refers to the resurrection of the dead and hence the resurrection of Jesus.

28:21 Paul's Jewish accusers in Jerusalem have not bothered to make contact with the Jews in Rome. Thus no accusation against him is known in Rome, which is beneficial to him and to the gospel. Were the Jews in Jerusalem happy that Paul was out of the country and had they therefore abandoned his cause?

28:22 The Jews put 'your views' on a par with 'this sect'. This suggests that they are inclined not to believe Paul – yet they want to hear more!

28:23 Even in Rome Paul is able to speak unhindered and for a long time about Jesus and his kingdom! God uses his situation as a prisoner in a special way.

28:24 The usual effect of gospel proclamation to the Jews is division among them, see verse 29 (and cf. 14:1–2; 17:4–5; 18:5–6, and 19:8–9). Some accept Jesus, some do not.

28:25–28 Luke shows that the Jews walk away from Paul, not the other way round. He then makes Paul give a kind of retrospect on his entire ministry among the Jews. Just like Isaiah and Jesus before him, Paul is disappointed with the lack of fruit from his work. Like them, he utters a prophetic warning, but this is not a condemnation: if the Jews harden their hearts, God's word can no longer penetrate. Paul is using the prophetic word to warn them not to harden their hearts. Verse 28 is a call to understand what is going on.

The words Paul speaks here are remarkably close to Romans 11. God has not rejected his old people Israel (11:1–2), but they have hardened and do not want to hear the gospel (11:7, 25). Meanwhile, gentiles will hear it and make Israel jealous (11:11–12). Paul does not say more in Acts 28, but in Romans 11 he also writes about his hope for the future salvation of the Jews.

28:29 (see NIV note). These words are probably a later addition which does not add much to verse 25.

28:30 Luke refers to a fixed period of two years, after which there was probably a decision taken about the fate of Paul. However, we do not know what that decision entailed.

28:31 The last words of the book are masterful: 'With all boldness and without hindrance'. In other words, the gospel is being freely proclaimed in the capital city of the world, and who will stop it?! 'With all boldness' is an incentive for faithful readers to be just as bold, while 'without hindrance' can be seen as a suggestion to the government not to hinder proclamation of the gospel.

Application

For us, the open end of Acts is a challenge. What prevents us from speaking boldly about Jesus? Luke invites us to write chapter 29 ourselves as it were. Over time there have been various organisations and activities under the name 'Acts 29'. In the 1950 years since Luke wrote his book, the world has obviously changed beyond recognition and the gospel has now reached the ends of the earth (1:8). In our part of the world it is hard to reach post-Christian people, but Jesus' command to do so remains in force and we have the freedom to carry it out.

For Thought and Discussion

1. Luke shows how deeply the Jews are divided over who Jesus is. In fact Luke is describing a very tragic situation. The gentiles are just as divided. From both groups some people come to faith in Jesus and some do not. Do you think that this is an accurate description of the situation?

2. Once again Paul goes to the Jews first, and this could annoy some of us. The priority of the Jews is one of the sharp edges of the gospel. According to Romans 11, we as Christians from the gentiles are merely grafted branches of God's tree. Can we accept this situation?

3. How would you explain the way Paul approaches the Jews to a Christian from a Muslim background?

4. In *The Message*[2] the last sentence of Acts is 'His door was always open'. What opportunities do you have to share Jesus with others? Are you contributing to the writing of Acts 29?

5. Are the Jewish people still a target group for our gospel proclamation? If not, why not? If so, how do we best approach them?

6. In the NIV the heading over the last section of Acts is 'Paul preaches at Rome under guard'. Any comments?

---

[2] Eugene H. Peterson, *The Message: The Bible in Contemporary Language* (Colorado Springs: NavPress, 2002).

Bibliography

Those who want to study Acts in more depth may turn to the following books:

Alexander, Loveday, *Acts*. The People's Bible Commentary (Oxford: Bible Reading Fellowship, 2006)

Fernando, Ajith, *Acts*. NIV Application Commentary (London: Hodder and Stoughton, 1998)

Marshall, I. Howard, *Acts: An Introduction and Commentary.* Tyndale New Testament Commentaries (Nottingham: IVP, 1980 and many reprints)

Milne, Bruce, *The Acts of the Apostles.* Focus on the Bible (Fearn, Ross-shire: Christian Focus Publications, 2010)

Other Books by Dr Pieter J. Lalleman

The Acts of John: a two-stage initiation into Johannine Gnosticism. Studies on the Apocryphal Acts of the Apostles, 4 (Leuven: Peeters, 1998)

The Lion and the Lamb: Studies on the Book of Revelation (London: Faithbuilders, 2016)

Enduring Treasure. The Lasting Value of the Old Testament for Christians (London: Faithbuilders, 2017)

With Martin H. Manser, David Barratt and Julius Steinberg, *Critical Companion to the Bible. A Literary Reference.* Facts on File Library of World Literature (New York: Facts on File, 2009)

Editor, *Challenging to change: dialogues with a radical Baptist theologian. Essays presented to Dr Nigel G. Wright on his sixtieth birthday* (London: Spurgeon's College, 2009)

Editor (with Peter J. Morden and Anthony R. Cross), *Grounded in Grace. Essays to Honour Ian M. Randall* (London: Spurgeon's College / Didcot: The Baptist Historical Society, 2013)

Editor (with Pierre Berthoud), *The Reformation. Its Roots and Its Legacy* (Eugene OR: Pickwick, 2017)

A book on the use of the Old Testament in the New Testament is in preparation for 2019.

www.ingramcontent.com/pod-product-compliance
Lightning Source LLC
Chambersburg PA
CBHW070324100426
42743CB00011B/2555